RUBY FALLS

FRONT COVER: The thundering waterfall in Ruby Falls Cavern is the tallest and deepest underground waterfall open to the public in the United States. (Courtesy of Ruby Falls, LLC.)

UPPER BACK COVER: These are some of the formations inside Ruby Falls Cavern. (Courtesy of Ruby Falls, LLC.)

LOWER BACK COVER: From left to right are the Mirror Pool, guests enjoying the waterfall, and Ruby Falls Cavern Castle. (Courtesy of Ruby Falls, LLC.)

Images of Modern America

RUBY FALLS

RUBY FALLS, LLC
FOREWORD BY JEANNE CRAWFORD

ARCADIA
PUBLISHING

Copyright © 2019 by Ruby Falls, LLC
ISBN 978-1-4671-2991-6

Published by Arcadia Publishing
Charleston, South Carolina

Printed in the United States of America

Library of Congress Control Number: 2019934923

For all general information, please contact Arcadia Publishing:
Telephone 843-853-2070
Fax 843-853-0044
E-mail sales@arcadiapublishing.com
For customer service and orders:
Toll-Free 1-888-313-2665

Visit us on the Internet at www.arcadiapublishing.com

CONTENTS

FOREWORD

This book tenderly pulls at my heart-strings. My grandfather Leo Lambert discovered Ruby Falls. Grandpa Leo looked at clouds and saw visions and possibilities. He was a thinker and dreamer who adored his love, my grandmother Ruby Losey. Grandpa followed her to Chattanooga when her family moved to the area from Indiana, and they married in 1916. As a chemist, his life's work was in a laboratory, but his dreams changed the course of the life he and Ruby created together.

Long ago, at a Sunday school class picnic on the river, Leo and Ruby learned about a cave system with an incredible history. The railroad had sealed off access to the caves, making them inaccessible. The picnic marked the very beginning of Leo's 10-year quest to open the caves. During the years of planning and securing financial backing, he worked for the US government in Illinois and Colorado. He developed a plan to drill down 420 feet through solid limestone to create a shaft for an elevator that would become the entry point for the long-sealed caves.

In 1928, Leo's vision finally broke ground, and excavation began for the elevator shaft. After drilling 260 feet below the surface of Lookout Mountain, the crew discovered a jagged hole inside the mountain. Through that small opening, Leo discovered a previously unknown natural treasure. In his wisdom, Leo Lambert wrote that the discovery was "a God thing." There were no more cracks or openings in the 420-foot deep shaft. Think of it—a hidden jewel, known only to God, found in the heart of Lookout Mountain. Grandpa Leo said he was "just a little proud" that God used him as the instrument to discover this jewel and make it known to the world.

Ruby Falls was discovered because Leo Lambert loved well. When he followed Ruby to Chattanooga, he had no idea what was ahead for him. He had never even been to Chattanooga. As in all love stories, true love is the final destination. Thus it was with Ruby and Leo Lambert. This was their love and life story's final destination.

Our family is proud that Leo's vision on that long-ago riverside picnic became a beloved destination and part of Chattanooga's heritage.

As Grandpa used to say: "Why, this is just the bee's knees!"

With love,
Jeanne Whisler Crawford

Acknowledgments

This book was lovingly compiled by past and current Ruby Falls team members. We would particularly like to thank the following people for their hard work and dedication to this project: Hollie Baranick, Jeanne Crawford, Ronnie Burk, Kara Van Brunt, Lara Holden Caughman, Beth Robinson, Neil Howard, Ray Zimmerman, Kent Ballew, Bob White, Hugh Morrow, Carlin McRae, Melissa Wagner, Brent Wade, Michael Brinkley, Roy Davis, Nick Skierra, Matt Owens, Britney Felker, the Day Ruhlman family, Diane Mallow Brown, Drew Thackston, Kayla Johnson, Libby Johnson, Albert Borum, David "Boomer" Brown, and Dustin Lindberg.

Unless otherwise noted, all images appear courtesy of Ruby Falls, LLC.

INTRODUCTION

It was an unlikely chemist from Indiana who ushered in a new age of exploration with an accidental discovery deep within Lookout Mountain. The discovery of Ruby Falls in Chattanooga, Tennessee, and the legacy it created are both remarkable and endearing. It is a tale of unlikely odds, love, and determination.

The story begins with a young man following his heart. Leo Lambert and Ruby Losey began dating as high school classmates in Gary, Indiana. After graduation, Leo was working as a chemist when Ruby moved with her family to Chattanooga, Tennessee. After a short time apart, Leo decided to follow Ruby and relocated to Chattanooga, where the couple married in 1916. Continuing his work as a chemist, Leo enjoyed exploring his new surroundings.

Leo learned of the rich history and folklore surrounding a local cave visible from the Tennessee River. Lookout Mountain Cave was well known to locals through centuries of use, first by Native Americans, followed by later visits for clandestine meetings, then as a hospital during the Civil War, and a legendary hideout for moonshine runners. Leo was dismayed to find only the first 20 feet of the cave was publicly accessible. In 1905, Southern Railroad Company intersected the cave to build a much-needed railway tunnel through Lookout Mountain, closing off the remainder of the cave. Driven by his desire for all to have access to explore and learn from its distinguished history, Leo was determined to re-open Lookout Mountain Cave.

After spending years researching various methods to access the cave, Leo came to an unusual solution in 1928 and traveled back to Indiana to share his plan with potential investors. The investors agreed to fund Leo's plan to excavate an elevator shaft descending 420 feet into the solid limestone of Lookout Mountain, giving access to the long-sealed cave.

With financing secured, Leo bought the land above Lookout Mountain Cave and excavators began drilling the shaft in the fall of 1928. Progress was slow but steady as crews drilled around the clock, removing five feet of limestone every 24 hours. In late December, the team was 260 feet into the mountain when they hit a void in the rock and felt a rush of air escape.

The workers excitedly called the Lambert home, leaving an urgent but vague message with Leo's young daughter. Leo rushed to the excavation site thinking something terrible had occurred. After arriving, he quickly realized the opposite. The 18-inch tall, five-foot wide opening in the rock was a passage to the unknown inside the mountain.

The following day, December 30, 1928, Leo led a small group of explorers into the darkness through the tight opening. By the time they emerged from the opening 17 hours later, Ruby was certain that Leo and the others had met their deaths. Instead, Leo returned exhausted and exhilarated by what they had discovered hidden inside the mountain.

Leo enthusiastically recounted how they crawled on their bellies inside a confining passage for six hours before the tunnel opened to a place where they could stand. They explored sections of the cavern with flowing underground streams and remarkable active geological formations. Moving further into the cavern, they heard the distant sound of rushing water. Following the sound, Leo hurried forward, falling when the floor elevation dropped beneath his feet. A thick layer of mud cushioned his landing. After picking himself up, the now dimming light of his carbide lamp reflected off a glimmer of falling water. Once the others made their way into the passage, their combined lights could just make out a plunging waterfall right in front of them. Eager to report on their findings, the group slowly made their way back to the anxious group assembled aboveground.

Several days later, Leo returned to the newfound cave with Ruby and christened this natural waterfall in her honor, naming it Ruby Falls. Drilling continued to the 420-foot mark, where the shaft intersected Lookout Mountain Cave as expected, 90 days after drilling had begun. Plans were made to open Ruby Falls Cavern for tours. Its passageways would be carefully widened, and the elevator would provide access to both Lookout Mountain Cave and Ruby Falls Cavern.

In total, 15,000 pounds of dynamite was used to loosen five million pounds of limestone, which was then removed one large bucket load at a time through the shaft. The excavated limestone was used to build Ruby Falls Cavern Castle.

With the trail through the new-found Ruby Falls Cavern still under construction, Lookout Mountain Cave opened to the public 14 months after drilling began on December 30, 1929. It had taken more than a decade for Leo's improbable dream to be realized. The cave that captured his attention forever changed the trajectory of his life.

On June 16, 1930, Ruby Falls Cavern opened for guided tours. Touring both Lookout Mountain Cave and Ruby Falls Cavern was an all-day outing, with most visitors bringing a picnic lunch to enjoy under the trees surrounding the castle. Sadly, Lookout Mountain Cave had been affected by decades of soot buildup from nearby train engines. Over time, the beauty and popularity of Ruby Falls overshadowed Lookout Mountain Cave. Tours through Lookout Mountain Cave were eventually phased out.

During the Depression, ownership of the cave passed from Leo Lambert; however, he remained involved for many years in various capacities during a long cycle of ownership changes. John T. Steiner Sr., the last owner of Ruby Falls, placed the company into a family trust in 2007.

Over half a million guests visit Ruby Falls annually, making it one of the most visited caves in the United States. Continuing Leo's mission, Ruby Falls is committed to protecting and preserving the natural wonders of the cave for the education and enjoyment of generations to come. As the first attraction in the United States to earn certification from Green Globe, the respected worldwide standard for sustainability, Ruby Falls is a leader in tourism sustainability and environmentally-sensitive business practices. Solar power, electric vehicle charging stations, LED lighting, recycling, sourcing sustainable business products, and a 16,000-gallon rainwater collection system for irrigation are just a few of the ways sustainability is at the core of the company's business practices.

The 2018 debut of Ruby Falls's multimillion-dollar expansion celebrated the iconic destination's largest building project since the completion of the castle in 1929. Embracing the legacy earned over the last 90 years, Ruby Falls Cavern Castle and Ruby Falls Cavern are listed in the National Register of Historic Places. Recognized for its natural beauty, Ruby Falls has been named one of the "World's Best Underground Attractions" by MSN Lifestyle, one of the "11 Most Impressive Waterfalls in the United States" by USA Today, the "Most Beautiful Place in Tennessee" by Thrillist, and is in the "Top 10 Caves in the Nation" by USA Today.

One

DISCOVERY AND LOOKOUT MOUNTAIN CAVE

The discovery of Ruby Falls began with another cave rich in history and lore. Located 160 feet below Ruby Falls Cavern, Lookout Mountain Cave sheltered Native Americans, served as a hospital during the Civil War, and was rumored to be both a bootlegger's hideout and the location of at least one operational still during Prohibition. Generations of Chattanoogans have fond memories of exploring in and around the storied cave. (Courtesy of Ronnie Burk.)

The original entrance to Lookout Mountain Cave was just a few feet from busy railroad tracks tucked against the bottom of Lookout Mountain. By 1905, rail traffic increased substantially. To meet the growing demand, Southern Railroad Company built an additional line by creating a 3,500-foot tunnel through Lookout Mountain. While the original entrance could still be seen, the tunnel intersected the pathway into the cave, cutting off access.

Pictured here is the entrance of the railroad tunnel intersecting Lookout Mountain Cave. For a time, the Southern Railroad Company gave curious explorers, cave surveyors, and historians permission to access Lookout Mountain Cave through a doorway inside the newly created tunnel. Eventually, the doorway was sealed to discourage explorers from entering the dangerously active railroad tunnel.

According to legend, the seventh president of the United States, Andrew Jackson, left his signature in Lookout Mountain Cave while traveling from Washington, DC, to his home in Nashville. Legends and lore become embellished over time, and it remains unknown if the signature was carved by President Jackson, another man with the same name, or by someone pranking bygone-era cave explorers. The mystery is forever buried in Lookout Mountain.

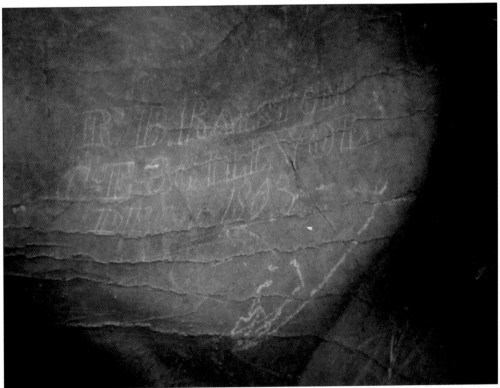

One of the most fascinating discoveries in Lookout Mountain Cave are the signatures covering the walls from the Civil War era, as well as signatures of explorers in the late 1800s and early 1900s. The earliest signatures were most likely made using smoke from carbon lights. Later signatures were scratched into the rock with knives and other sharp tools. Some signatures are just a name, others are very ornate, and many include a date.

Over centuries, a variety of animals found shelter inside Lookout Mountain Cave. Early expeditions revealed the remains of several animal species after explorers arduously crawled for hours through tight cavern passageways. Discoveries included the skull of a black bear, multiple sets of jaguar bones, hellbender salamander remains, and even a chicken. The remains were sent to several universities to be analyzed and verified. Scientific evaluation dated the jaguar bones to the Pleistocene era and determined that the animals entered the cave through a more accessible opening that was lost over time due to natural circumstances. The bear skull and a plaster cast of the jaguar bones have been preserved by Ruby Falls. (Above, courtesy of Ronnie Burk.)

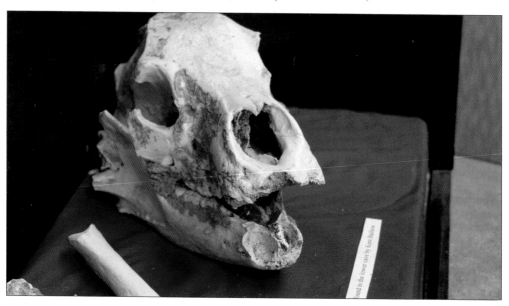

Some of the most curious artifacts in Lookout Mountain Cave include 13 stone boxes found together in one section. Early tour guides speculated about the origin and purpose of these mysterious boxes. Some believed that whatever was placed inside the boxes was meant to be sealed and hidden, with the intention of unsealing the boxes privately. Others concluded that a type of voting event took place here, with the boxes used for ballot collection. Either theory is plausible and may explain the purpose of the holes at the top of the box. The origin, purpose, and originators of the square stone boxes remain a mystery.

Leo Bragg Lambert sits on his 1920s Excelsior-Henderson Super X motorcycle. Leo followed his sweetheart, Ruby, to Chattanooga, Tennessee, from Gary, Indiana. The young chemist received permission from the railroad company to explore Lookout Mountain Cave. Leo's newfound fascination with the cave changed the trajectory of his life. (Courtesy of Jeanne Crawford.)

Leo dreamed of sharing the history of Lookout Mountain Cave by opening it to the public for tours. He determined that the sealed cave could be accessed from above if an elevator shaft could be excavated deep into the mountain. He rallied a team of investors and secured $250,000 in financial backing to fulfill his vision to reopen the cave.

When Leo Lambert emerged from his 17-hour journey inside the dark cave, only his boots and helmet could be saved. Ruby burned the rest of the clothing he had worn because their stench was overwhelming, and the clothes were beyond redemption. The boots and helmet are on display at a gift shop on Lookout Mountain owned by Jeanne Crawford, Leo and Ruby Lambert's granddaughter.

Leo Lambert crawls through an underground stream in Ruby Falls Cave. After his discovery of Ruby Falls, he remained an avid caver and helped develop tours for other caves in the area such as Raccoon Mountain Cavern and Nickajack Cave. (Courtesy of Jeanne Crawford.)

Ruby Eugenia Losey was Leo Lambert's high school sweetheart. In 1915, she moved with her family from Gary, Indiana, to Chattanooga, Tennessee. Her father, a professional photographer, was commissioned to photograph the 6th Cavalry and other troops stationed at Fort Oglethorpe. In Chattanooga, Ruby had opportunities to perform at the Tivoli Theater singing opera and playing the organ before an audience. (Courtesy of Jeanne Crawford.)

Ruby was adventurous enough to go with Leo Lambert into Ruby Falls Cavern, yet she also adhered to many cultural and social traditions for women. When she played tennis with Leo, she never moved from her spot, believing it was Leo's job to hit the ball to her. Her opera glasses, handbag, and tennis shoes are on display next to Leo's boots and helmet.

Leo and Ruby's love story has delighted Ruby Falls guests for close to 100 years. Ruby regaled visitors with stories of Leo stealing her hymn book at their church in Indiana, making her "so mad until the day it didn't." It was a bold choice for Leo to follow Ruby and her family to Chattanooga, but the decision proved wise. Leo and Ruby married on August 16, 1916, at Ridgedale Methodist Church. Three of their eight children survived to adulthood. Together, they faced sorrow and financial challenges along with happy times. Ruby was devastated when Leo died. When she passed away less than a year later, the doctor reportedly suggested that she had died of a broken heart. (Courtesy of Jeanne Crawford.)

Leo contracted the services of Salmon & Cowan Inc., one of the country's leading mining engineering firms, to excavate the elevator shaft. Drilling began November 1, 1928. Progress was tediously slow but steady. Work continued around the clock, with three teams each working an eight-hour shift daily. The limestone removed from the elevator shaft was used to construct Ruby Falls Cavern Castle and Lookout Mountain Tower.

In late December 1928, Tillman Hodge was operating a jackhammer in the elevator shaft. He uncovered a void in the rock and felt a gust of air. The small opening appeared to lead into an underground passage. The excited crew attempted to reach Leo Lambert by phone. Discovering he was not at home, they left a message with his young daughter to call them when he came home due to a "happening" in the elevator shaft. By the time Leo got the message, his daughter had led him to believe that someone was badly hurt or dead. Lambert jumped into his vehicle and sped 35 miles per hour down Broad Street to the site.

Leo led a small group of explorers into the darkness through the tight gap. By the time he and the group emerged from the opening 17 hours later, Ruby was certain they had met their death. Instead, Leo returned exhausted and exhilarated by what they had found hidden inside the mountain. (Courtesy of Jeanne Crawford.)

After excavation was completed, crews spent 11 months erecting the steel frame of the shaft. Starting 420 feet below ground in Lookout Mountain Cave, the crew worked their way up the shaft. While structural work for the elevator continued, electricians installed lighting throughout Lookout Mountain Cave. A narrow pathway was carefully excavated leading to the waterfall in Ruby Falls Cavern. The extensive pathway project delayed the beginning of Ruby Falls tours until June 1930.

Leo recounted how he and the crew crawled inside a passage for six hours before the tunnel opened to a place where they could stand. They explored cavern areas with underground streams and active geological formations. As Leo hurried toward the sound of rushing water, he fell when the floor elevation dropped beneath him. The dimming light of his lamp reflected off a glimmer of falling water. Once the others made their way into the passage, their combined lights could just make out part of a plunging waterfall. Days later, Leo returned to the waterfall with Ruby, sharing his plans to name it in her honor.

Stonemasons used the limestone removed from the elevator shaft to build the exterior walls of Ruby Falls Cavern Castle and Lookout Mountain Tower. Designed by architect R.H. Hunt, the castle was modeled after a 15th-century Irish castle. The iconic landmark was listed in the National Register of Historic Places in 1986.

Having had the waterfall named after her, Ruby was determined to make her mark on the castle as well. The original design of the front steps was to descend straight down to the drive. Ruby insisted that the architect change his design to create curved steps, making the entrance more welcoming and graceful. She also planted roses on the side of the castle for visitors to enjoy. (Courtesy of Jeanne Crawford.)

One of the earliest Ruby Falls guest photographs was taken in the waterfall room known as Solomon's Temple. While Lookout Mountain Cave tours began in December 1929, work continued in Ruby Falls Cavern for six more months before it opened to the public. Existing pathways were carefully enlarged, creating walkable access through the cave, including sections that previously required crawling. Lighting was added to the cavern trail and waterfall. On June 16, 1930, Ruby Falls Cavern opened for tours. Eventually, Ruby Falls became more popular than Lookout Mountain Cave because of an abundance of formations and the enormous waterfall. In 1935, scheduled Lookout Mountain Cave tours were phased out, with only occasional tours available through 1955. (Courtesy of Jeanne Crawford.)

Two

RUBY FALLS HISTORY

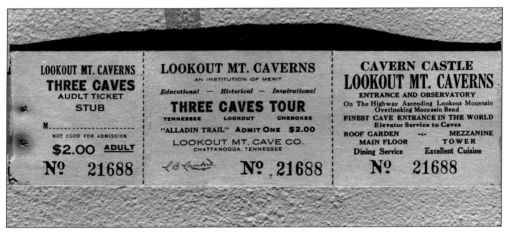

LOOKOUT MT. CAVERNS	LOOKOUT MT. CAVERNS	CAVERN CASTLE
THREE CAVES	AN INSTITUTION OF MERIT	**LOOKOUT MT. CAVERNS**
AUDLT TICKET	*Educational — Historical — Inspirational*	ENTRANCE AND OBSERVATORY
STUB	**THREE CAVES TOUR**	On The Highway Ascending Lookout Mountain Overlooking Moccasin Bend
M----------------------------	TENNESSEE LOOKOUT CHEROKEE	FINEST CAVE ENTRANCE IN THE WORLD Elevator Service to Caves
NOT GOOD FOR ADMISSION	"ALLADIN TRAIL" ADMIT ONE $2.00	ROOF GARDEN -:- MEZZANINE
	LOOKOUT MT. CAVE CO.	MAIN FLOOR TOWER
$2.00 **ADULT**	CHATTANOOGA. TENNESSEE	Dining Service Excellent Cuisine
№ 21688	*L B Lombard.* № 21688	№ 21688

When both Ruby Falls Cavern and Lookout Mountain Cave were open for tours, a visit was an all-day event. Lookout Mountain Cave was separated into two tours. Combined with Ruby Falls Cavern, visitors had the opportunity to tour all three caves for $2. Guests would enjoy a tour or two, then spread out on the castle grounds for a picnic lunch or purchase lunch from the café inside the castle. After a leisurely meal, they would finish their tours.

The castle quickly became a treasured part of Chattanooga. Originally featuring two stories and an impressive tower, the stone building overlooked the Tennessee Valley, downtown Chattanooga, and the Tennessee River. Early advertisements boasted that it was the most beautiful cavern entrance in the world. In 1973, a third floor was added to house Ruby Falls Treetops gift shop.

When the castle opened in 1930, the lobby featured a large stone fireplace. It was later obscured when a staircase was added to allow easier access to the second floor. The lobby served multiple functions: as an area for guests to gather before their tour, a café serving lunch and dinner, and a dance floor on Friday and Saturday evenings. Private dining rooms were available on the mezzanine.

The original ticket desk was outfitted with an oversized brass cash register that remained in use until the 1960s. The register became known as "burglar proof" when longtime employee Mack Nelson caught two men attempting to steal it. Known for always having his trusty shotgun on him, Nelson caught them unaware. One burglar ran away. Nelson held the other at gunpoint, forcing the would-be thief to hold the massive register until the police arrived.

The original elevator was a manually operated freight elevator with a throttle instead of buttons and was powered by gasoline. The only way to access Ruby Falls Cavern and Lookout Mountain Cave was with the elevator. It made a stop at Ruby Falls Cavern, 260 feet below the castle, and then descended an additional 160 feet to Lookout Mountain Cave. The elevator was capable of reaching both caves until 1998, when it was decided to permanently close Lookout Mountain Cave.

Bill and Bessie Mallow, pictured with their son Edward Mallow, visited from Chillicothe, Ohio, in the early 1940s. After touring the caves, guests were welcome to roam the grounds, picnic, and enjoy the view from the property. (Courtesy of Diane Mallow Brown.)

In the mid-1930s, a promotional event at Ruby Falls was sponsored by a local ice company. Blocks of ice were placed near the waterfall, highlighting the cool cavern temperature compared to the summer heat. A sales clerk at a retail shop in Chattanooga, Gay Wasson Day was selected to model the shop's swimwear at the event. (Courtesy of the Gay Day Ruhlman family, Suzanne Ruhlman Prigohzy.)

Tours to Lookout Mountain Cave continued until 1955. What it lacked in formations it made up for in rich history. Combined with the unique folklore that tour guides contributed, touring the two different levels of the cave was a very pleasant way to spend an afternoon, provided one did not mind a little soot coming in through the train tunnel. Tours of Lookout Mountain Cave eventually stopped due to the overwhelming popularity of Ruby Falls. (Right, courtesy of Jeanne Crawford.)

The multilevel Lookout Mountain Cave was accessed through a combination of straight and spiral staircases. Intricate, winding tunnels such as the Serpentine Trail were created by water eroding the rock. Only a small section of Lookout Mountain Cave was accessible to tours. Six miles of cave had been identified by 1929, but spelunkers speculated that the cave contained far more than what had been explored. The area of the cave included on the tour had pathways and wooden bridges for easier passage, with light bulbs hanging from electric wires along the path.

One of the most memorable celebrity visitors was Babe Ruth, who toured the caves in April 1931 when the Yankees traveled to Chattanooga to play an exhibition game against the Chattanooga Lookouts. The game was especially memorable because female pitcher Jackie Mitchell struck out both Ruth and Lou Gehrig back to back. Note the laughing men in the back. Leo Lambert (at left), being short, quickly jumped up to the top step before the picture was taken to appear to stand eye to eye with six-foot-two Babe Ruth.

A bridge was built around the waterfall in 1954, giving guests the opportunity to walk behind the falls. The bridge remains in place; however, for safety reasons, access was closed in 2012. Guests fondly remember the unusual view from the back of the falls. Cavers consider it good luck if you are touched by drops of water in a cave. Called a "cave kiss" by Ruby Falls tour guides, guests have plenty of opportunities to test the theory.

There were two major explorations above the waterfall in the 1950s and 1960s. Leo Lambert and his son-in-law Paul Whistler were in the process of designing a ladder to reach the top of the falls when Leo unexpectedly passed away. Paul completed the project and led the first major exploration above the waterfall in Leo's honor. (Courtesy of Jeanne Crawford.)

The second, more lengthy expedition above the falls involved constructing scaffolding to reach the top of the waterfall and climbing a rope ladder to enter the section of the cave above the falls. (Courtesy of Ronnie Burk.)

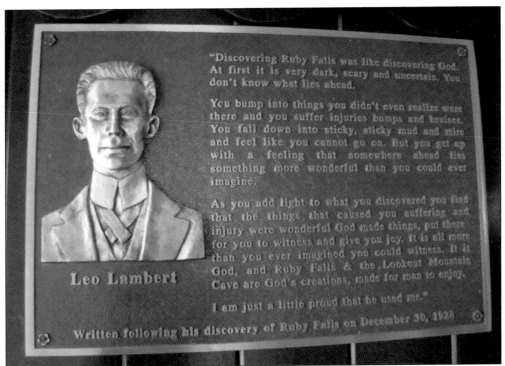

"Discovering Ruby Falls was like discovering God. At first it is very dark, scary and uncertain. You don't know what lies ahead.

You bump into things you didn't even realize were there and you suffer injuries bumps and bruises. You fall down into sticky, sticky mud and mire and feel like you cannot go on. But you get up with a feeling that somewhere ahead lies something more wonderful than you could ever imagine.

As you add light to what you discovered you find that the things that caused you suffering and injury were wonderful God made things, put there for you to witness and give you joy. It is all more than you ever imagined you could witness. It is God, and Ruby Falls & the Lookout Mountain Cave are God's creations, made for man to enjoy.

I am just a little proud that he used me."

Leo Lambert

Written following his discovery of Ruby Falls on December 30, 1928.

Years after Leo Lambert's death, his family discovered a profound passage in his journal about finding Ruby Falls. On the 80th anniversary of the discovery of Ruby Falls, a bronze plaque dedicated to Lambert was placed on the front porch of the castle. Its inscription shares the reflective journal entry.

In 1986, Ruby Falls Cavern, the castle, and Lookout Mountain Cave were listed in the National Register of Historic Places in recognition of their transformational impact on early tourism and economic development in the Chattanooga area. Ruby Falls has grown to become a major tourist destination in the Southeast, adding millions of dollars annually to the region's economy.

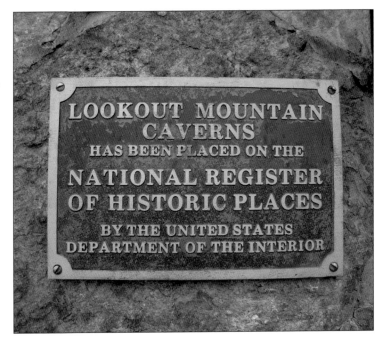

LOOKOUT MOUNTAIN CAVERNS HAS BEEN PLACED ON THE NATIONAL REGISTER OF HISTORIC PLACES BY THE UNITED STATES DEPARTMENT OF THE INTERIOR

The top of Lookout Mountain Tower was not open to guests when Ruby Falls Cavern Castle opened in 1929. The castle's rooftop garden above the second floor was designated for Friday and Saturday night dances and other special events. In 1974, outdoor stairs were added, giving guests access to the top of the tower and its phenomenal view of the Tennessee Valley, Cumberland Plateau, and the winding Tennessee River.

Early tours of Ruby Falls Cavern also included the tucked-away segment of the cave now only open during special events. Originally, the pathway through this section stretched a few hundred feet, ending with a locked gate blocking access to the rugged section of the passage. In 1974, Ruby Falls began excavation to build a tunnel beyond the gate. The tunnel would lead to a newly created exit on Scenic Highway, providing a much-anticipated alternate way to access and exit the cave. (Courtesy of Ronnie Burk.).

When the tunnel excavation project was finished, the new secondary cave exit was secured by locking steel doors visible on the side of Lookout Mountain. A metal building was added outside the doors in 2004, creating a vestibule to protect the exit from harsh weather and would-be trespassers. Ruby Falls's award-winning Haunted Cavern was located in this section of the cave from 2004 to 2016. (Courtesy of Ronnie Burk.).

Visitors on the Ruby Falls tour were fascinated with the natural sights, including stalactites, stalagmites, and other formations throughout the cave. The Onyx Column continues to grow in the Onyx Jungle passageway, one of the cave's most active sections.

Many guests visiting Ruby Falls had never witnessed ancient geological formations like those found scattered throughout the cave. The beautiful Crystal Chandelier and Totem Pole were showcased on a popular postcard.

"Ladies and gentlemen, we now have a tour leaving for Ruby Falls. For those of you with tickets, please step down this way." Tour guides made this announcement in the lobby of the cavern castle for 88 years, gathering guests for the next tour at the entrance of the elevator. Before timed-entry tickets were introduced in 2018, guests waited in line up to three hours on peak-attendance days, with the tour queue extending out the castle doors and several hundred feet into the parking lot.

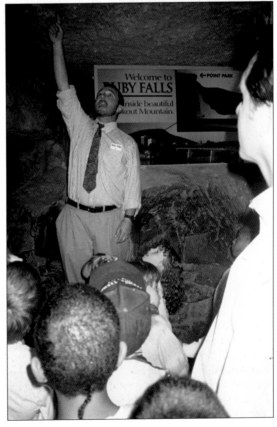

For guest safety, cave access has always been provided only with a guided tour. Initial tours were inconsistent in their length and content, with some lasting up to four hours. Today, the Ruby Falls Classic Waterfall Tour is offered daily, and specialty tours are scheduled on select days. Many longtime guides with years of service make such a lasting impression that guests ask for the same guide again on their next visit.

Employee Chuck Mumea takes his turn operating the elevator. At the time, a yellow painted line marked the spot in the shaft where the operator should slow down to reach the ground level. Today, the elevator is computer controlled, with clear glass doors instead of the barred, open-air door, allowing guests to safely view the solid stone shaft. (Courtesy of Ronnie Burk.)

A sign next to the elevator entrance reads "Fallout Shelter." In the 1960s, Ruby Falls Cavern was designated the first fallout shelter in the Chattanooga area, with a capacity of 720 people. Drums of water and dehydrated food were tucked away in the cave.

Former Ruby Falls manager Ronnie Burk presents the history of Lookout Mountain and the surrounding area to guests gathered to begin their tour. Tour guides pointed to specific areas on the map as an audio recording played and various sections of the map were illuminated. (Courtesy of Ronnie Burk.)

Longtime employee Bob White stands in what was known as the Map Room. State-of-the art when it launched, the Map Room featured twinkling lights illustrating the path of water through the cave, eventually joining the Tennessee River. The show was later replaced with two 55-inch monitors in the early 2000s showing a short film about the discovery of Ruby Falls.

Guests return year after year with their children, grandchildren, and great-grandchildren. Frequently returning guests include parents bringing their children to see where they got engaged, grandparents sharing memories of their honeymoon with children and grandchildren, and multi-generation family reunions revisiting Ruby Falls to introduce the fourth and fifth generations to the wonders hidden underground. These return guests are cherished by the team.

A tour guide introduces herself to a school group before watching a presentation on the history of Ruby Falls. Many tour guides at Ruby Falls had their first experience of the cave while on a local school group tour, and many guests reminisce about their first encounter of Ruby Falls being with a school group.

Springtime from the 1980s to early 2000s was nicknamed "bus season." Students and tour groups from all over the world came to Ruby Falls each spring. Today, Ruby Falls is proud to welcome school groups and tour destination groups year-round.

In the late 1980s to early 1990s, Spunky the Spelunkasaurus appeared on school-focused promotional materials. To educate students about the geology and nature of caves, lesson plans were mailed to area schools featuring the geology of Ruby Falls Cavern. Special tours were created for visiting school groups.

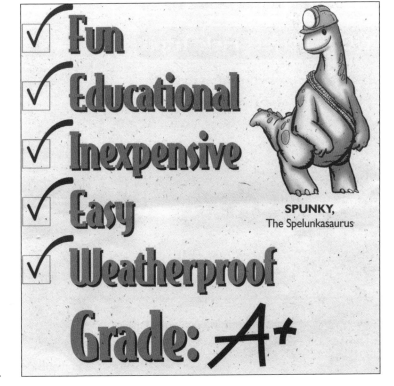

✓ Fun
✓ Educational
✓ Inexpensive
✓ Easy
✓ Weatherproof

Grade: A+

SPUNKY,
The Spelunkasaurus

In the late 1980s, Ruby Falls president Jack T. Steiner Sr. worked with designers to build an expansive deck off the third floor of the castle. It included a new eatery, arcade, and playground featuring the newest concept in outdoor play. The playground's creator, Jack Pentes, was a theme park designer and inventor of "soft contained play." Pentes was renowned for his whimsical playgrounds popping up at fast-food restaurants across the nation.

The new deck and venues were completed in 1990 and named Fun Forest. Visitors loved being able to extend their visit, giving their children a chance to run off some energy on the playground before going back to their cars. The playground's ball pit was a favorite spot. Even though the ball pit was removed in the late 1990s, balls have been found around the property as recently as 2018.

Fun Forest went through several renovations. The top area of the playground was removed to allow covered seating with a beautiful view of the Chattanooga area. The arcade was torn down and replaced with a gemstone panning sluice. Guests could pan for gemstones or fossils. The deck was popular for birthday parties and evening receptions, where guest seated above the playground could take in the exceptional view.

An essential photo opportunity for visitors has always been the My Trip Thru Ruby Falls archways. Located on opposite sides of the castle for years, the two separate structures are the site of millions of memories from family visits, first dates, group outings, and more. During the 2017–2018 expansion projects, one of the arches was carefully wrapped and safely moved, while its twin remains in its original location. The removed arch will be reinstalled on the property in 2021.

Frank Tramble worked as a parking attendant for many years. Much like today, Ruby Falls parking attendants directed guests into the parking lot and waved to local residents as they drove by the castle. Ruby Falls placed billboards near the road by the property entrance to direct traffic to the caves and Lookout Mountain Tower. The signs and attendants were popular with the locals and tourists, many of whom would comment on how it would brighten their day to see the staff members smile and wave as they drove past. (Courtesy of Ronnie Burk.)

The street entrance to Ruby Falls was upgraded in late 2002, when Ruby Falls president John T. "Jack" Steiner commissioned a fountain to be built beside Scenic Highway. Since then, the fountain has become an iconic fixture at Ruby Falls. Thousands of visitors take their picture in front of the fountain each year. It has become a landmark for citizens of Lookout Mountain, easily seen by residents and visitors alike while driving up the mountain.

The John Thomas Steiner Sr. Memorial Scholarship was established in 2008 to honor the memory of the former Ruby Falls president. It recognizes staff members who demonstrate commitment and passion for their studies, community, and careers. Movita Steiner (second from right), the widow of the late Jack Steiner Sr., is pictured with 2018 scholarship recipients (from left to right) Ashli Brotherton, Farin Cloyd, and Clayton Curole.

Ruby Falls was one of the first caves in the nation to introduce Wi-Fi underground. Calling the service SmartCave, guests can upload pictures to social media, check their email, and stay in touch with loved ones while they are deep within Lookout Mountain.

Road signs and billboards of all sizes marked the way to Ruby Falls. Outdoor advertising played a role in increasing the number of guests. With the introduction of the Highway Beautification Act in 1958, Ruby Falls was one of the first companies to take an active role in decreasing outdoor advertising along Scenic Highway, and led efforts to use advertising that was harmonious with the area's natural beauty.

While enjoying the wonderful views from the winding roads of Scenic Highway in the early 1930s, drivers witnessed the construction of Ruby Falls Cavern Castle. Once completed, billboards marked the entrance to Ruby Falls, enticing visitors to turn in and tour the caves. In 2002, the billboard was replaced with a water fountain.

In a dual advertising collaboration, Chattanooga's Price Auto Company photographed its stock of Durant Motors vehicles in front of the castle upon its completion. Ruby Falls founder Leo Lambert is second from the left. The Durant Motor Co. was established by former General Motors CEO William Durant and did not survive the Great Depression, closing in 1932.

Ruby Falls painted signs on barns along the major highways to help advertise the destination. This was a boon to the barn owners in the area, who would have their barns painted at the expense of Ruby Falls. Some of these barn signs can still be seen today.

With billboards contributing to its success, Ruby Falls expanded its holdings in the region. Landowners were given lifetime passes in addition to lease payments in exchange for rights to place a billboard on their property. From 1999 to 2018, Ruby Falls and Rock City jointly owned a billboard company. Ruby Falls acquired sole ownership in 2018, including its portfolio of 92 billboard assets in Tennessee, Georgia, Alabama, and North Carolina.

Parking attendants placed bumper tags on cars in the Ruby Falls parking lot while their owners toured the caverns. A precursor to modern bumper stickers, these tags were made of colorful, heavy cardboard, and connected to the bumper with wires. Between tours, the tour guides would thread wire through the tags to make it easier for the outside staff to slip them on. When cars began to have attached bumpers, the practice was discontinued.

When the Fun Forest playground opened, Ruby Falls partnered with area hotels to place a tent card in each room offering a free child's ticket. Featuring the playground, each tent card encouraged guests with children to spend part of their day at Ruby Falls.

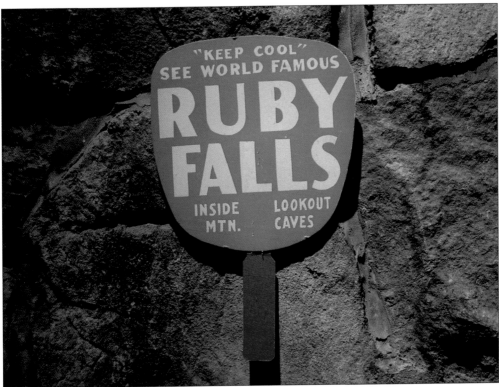

As business increased, the castle lobby was not large enough to hold all the guests waiting to take a tour. The lines for the ticket desk and elevator extended outside. With the Tennessee summer heat soaring, Ruby Falls handed out free souvenir fans to guests waiting in line.

In the late 1990s and early 2000s, Ruby Falls began a marketing campaign enticing schools to visit Ruby Falls. A resource guide was developed matching the local area's curriculum standards that included geology, history, and environmental education. An accompanying workbook included quizzes and activities, such as Grow Your Own Stalactite.

In Ruby Falls's early years, tours were available until 11:00 p.m. Today, tours are given until 8:00 p.m., with twilight hours on select summer nights. Lantern Tours are offered after hours on Friday nights, giving guests the opportunity to explore the cave with a guide using only the light of handheld lanterns. Scenic views are everywhere at Ruby Falls, thanks to its prime Lookout Mountain location. Guests can time their visit to take in pink-hued sunrises, midday cloud shadows on the Tennessee River, apricot sunsets, or star-filled night skies.

Three

GEOLOGY AND RUBY FALLS CAVERN

Located deep within Lookout Mountain, Ruby Falls is a geological wonder that has drawn visitors and scientists from around the world to explore its natural beauty. Ruby Falls Cavern is classified as a solution or karst cave. Originating from the Lookout Mountain watershed, the waterfall began from surface streams that flowed into the cavern through cracks and crevices across the mountain. Over millions of years, the flow of water carved through the limestone creating the dome room, also known as Solomon's Temple, where the spectacular Ruby Falls is on display. The defined layers of deposited sand and clay, also known as strata, are visible along the cave walls.

Ruby Falls Cavern is part of the naturally occurring watershed. Water flows through Lookout Mountain to the waterfall before making its way to a series of small underground streams, eventually joining the Tennessee River. Over thousands of years, through dissolution erosion, the flow of water carved out the dome room of the waterfall. Smooth areas of the limestone walls are evidence of the natural erosion process.

Visible on the side of Lookout Mountain, Ruby Falls Cavern Castle punctuates the majestic geological terrain of the Chattanooga area. When continents collided, the land was pushed upward to form mountains. At one point in history, Lookout Mountain was on the seabed floor of a shallow ocean. There are many types of sea fossils found in both the cave and surrounding area.

The growth rate of the formations in the cave is dependent on the mineral content of the water and amount of rainfall. The mineral content also affects the color of the formations. Appearing white in color, calcium is a very common mineral found in the limestone that forms the caverns of Ruby Falls. Large calcite draperies, stalagmites, and bell canopies can be found throughout the cave.

The stalactite formations found on the ceiling of Ruby Falls Cavern have been formed by water flowing through the limestone rock of the cave. The water drips through the cave ceiling depositing minerals, which build up over time to create stunning formations like the Crystal Chandelier.

Rising from the cave floor, stalagmites are formed when minerals are deposited by water dripping from the cave ceiling. Showcased on the Ruby Falls tour, Cactus and Candle is no longer a live formation, giving guests the opportunity to feel its smooth texture. The oils from the hands of guests are left behind, creating the smooth finish and luster. Touching other formations in the cave is prohibited, as it will affect their growth and natural appearance.

The Onyx Column is a wonderful example of a cave column. Formed when stalactites and stalagmites grow and fuse together, columns are found throughout Ruby Falls Cavern. Standing approximately six feet tall, the Onyx Column is the largest of this type of formation found in the cave and is still actively growing.

Soda straws found in Ruby Falls Cavern are hollow-tubed stalactites formed from calcium carbonate. These tubular stalactites grow at a much slower rate than a normal stalactite. Inspired by the huge number of soda straws along the ceiling, Leo and Ruby Lambert named this area of the cave the Hall of Dreams.

Drapery formations are the buildup of a solution of water and calcite as it flows along overhanging rock. As the atmosphere of a cave loses carbon dioxide, the solution becomes saturated and dry. The calcite does not become saturated and leaves behind a thin trail. When water begins to flow again, minerals are deposited along these trails, forming draperies. Angel's Wing is the narrowest drapery in Ruby Falls Cavern and is almost pure calcite.

Humorously referred to as the "north end of a south-bound donkey," the Donkey formation is a favorite among visitors. Tour-guide lore from the 1960s suggests that tour guide Brinkley lost a bet and rode a donkey to the waterfall and back as a publicity stunt. The story claims he named the donkey Jack and donated him to a local farm after riding.

Ruby Falls has several beautiful examples of bell canopy formations. Bell canopies are a form of flowstone, which can form over compacted dirt, mud, or clay. Over time, these materials can be washed away, leaving behind a bell-shaped formation.

The Leaning Tower is one of the most fascinating formations in the cave. It is a beautiful example of a bell canopy as well as a stalagmite and column. The initial rate of water flow caused a stalagmite to form. As the water rate changed, soda straws and stalactites began to grow, eventually reaching the stalagmite and creating a column.

Several pockets of helictites are found in Ruby Falls Cavern. These fascinating formations are a type of stalactite that seem to disobey the laws of gravity. The growth of helictites can branch and curl in any direction, creating the delicate formations.

Beautiful examples of flowstone formations are on display throughout Ruby Falls Cavern. Flowstone is formed when mineral-rich water flows across the floor or a downward slope in the cave. As the water descends the slope, it deposits minerals. The color of the formations is determined by different minerals found in the cave, such as iron and manganese.

The ceiling above the Mirror Pool is often referred to as the stalactite nursery due to the small and short nature of these stalactites. Interestingly, these formations are actually quite old. The growth rate of stalactites is very slow, averaging 1.9 inches every 100 years.

When Ruby Falls opened to the public in 1930, the United States had recently entered the Great Depression. During these difficult times, formations were broken and removed from the cave to be sold as a means of income. Since this time, damaging or removing formations from the cave has been strictly prohibited to protect the ancient speleothems. Fortunately, Ruby Falls is a living cave system, and new growth can be seen emerging from the previously damaged formations.

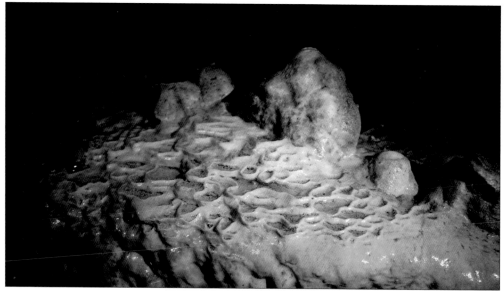

Rimstone is a common type of formation found in limestone caves created when water drips from the ceiling onto a surface with a slight slope. Groundwater permeates through small cracks in the rock above, dripping onto a surface where the formations begin to grow. Several rimstone calcite pools are visible near the Mirror Pool in Ruby Falls Cavern. These are the result of water rich in calcium carbonate. A close look reveals tiny calcite crystals forming along the inside edge of the pools. Other minerals found in the water in this area include trace amounts of sulfur, iron oxide, manganese, copper, calcium, and cobalt.

Ruby Falls is a calcite-rich cave. Calcite is a white or colorless mineral consisting of calcium carbonate. It is a major constituent of sedimentary rocks such as limestone, which is made up of ancient seashells. Calcite is the most stable polymorph of calcium carbonate. Ultraviolet light is used in the cave to showcase the calcite, creating a black-light effect.

There are many underground streams in Lookout Mountain. These streams divide and come together at multiple points, including the waterfall and other areas of Ruby Falls Cavern. The streams in Ruby Falls Cavern flow into the Tennessee River.

These gypsum needles on the cave floor were at one time full stalactites. As water rushed through the cave, it knocked these stalactites off the ceiling. Over time, water continued to drip from the ceiling, causing the gypsum needles to be fused to the cave floor.

Lookout Mountain Tower was constructed from limestone excavated from the elevator shaft in the 1920s. Several fossils can be seen in the tower rocks. While the types of fossils have not been officially confirmed, some speculate that they are plant or fish in origin.

Ruby Falls is open 364 days a year. The only exception to the operations schedule is in the event of heavy, persistent rain. Four to six inches of rainfall over a six- to eight-hour time will force the underground streams to rise, covering the walkways. When this happens, tours are temporarily stopped. Once flooding occurs, it can take 24 hours or longer for the water to recede below the walkways. When the water is cleared from the pathways, tours resume. Visiting immediately after a flood offers one of the most spectacular views of the waterfall due to the increased water flow. During these times, tour guides often struggle to be heard over the thundering sound of the falls.

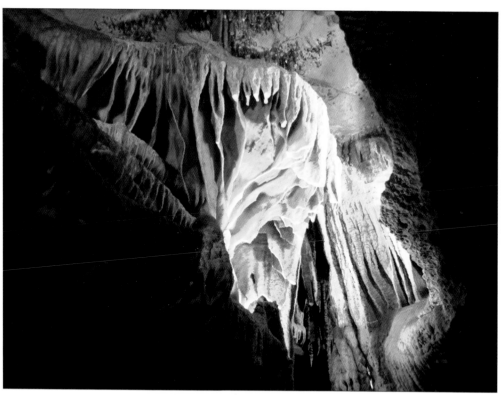

The intricate beauty of cave formations creates mystery and amazement throughout the Ruby Falls tour. Combinations of white calcium flowstone and drapery hidden in cave alcoves lend a natural splendor to the underground surface, reminding visitors that there is beauty and wonder in unexpected places.

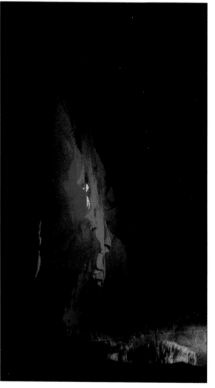

Ruby's Drapery is the longest drapery formation found in the cave. Measuring over six feet long, this beautiful wonder is tucked away in a high crevice of the cave. The delicate folds are emphasized by shining two different colors of lights on either side of the formation.

Four

HAPPENINGS AT RUBY FALLS

Ruby Falls is proud to host and sponsor community and private events benefitting local residents, current guests, and nonprofit organizations. From organized dances when Ruby Falls first opened in the 1930s to today's annual barbecue cook-off and holiday events, Ruby Falls continues to create memorable experiences for guests and the community.

Over the years, Ruby Falls has provided a unique wedding venue for many couples. The first ceremony held at Ruby Falls was on February 7, 1930, when Victor Peace and Louise Langley were married in Lookout Mountain Cave. The wedding officiant was Reverend Hounshell of Ridgedale Methodist Church. Incidentally, this was the same church where Leo and Ruby Lambert exchanged their vows. Today, Ruby Falls continues to be a popular location for marriage proposals and weddings. Most weddings take place at the waterfall, while some have been conducted on Lookout Mountain Tower and the surrounding grounds. Happy brides beam for the cameras, not minding the mud on the hems of their gowns for the chance to exchange vows in front of the iconic waterfall.

Investing in the local community has always been an important part of Ruby Falls. Over the years, Ruby Falls has sponsored area sports teams, academic competitions, theater and music performances, and intern programs.

In 1937, Ruby Falls sponsored Chattanooga Day, welcoming citizens of Chattanooga to visit for only 75¢, with children admitted free. In an effort to encourage area residents to bring their out-of-town friends and family to Ruby Falls, free resident passes were available during the 1990s and 2000.

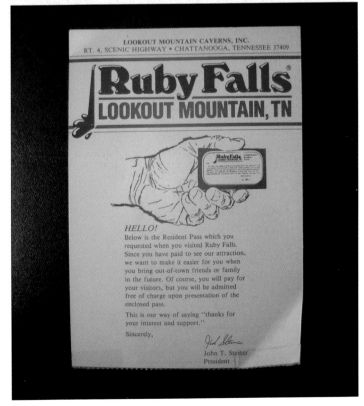

LOOKOUT MOUNTAIN CAVERNS, INC.
RT. 4, SCENIC HIGHWAY • CHATTANOOGA, TENNESSEE 37409

RubyFalls®
LOOKOUT MOUNTAIN, TN

HELLO!

Below is the Resident Pass which you requested when you visited Ruby Falls. Since you have paid to see our attraction, we want to make it easier for you when you bring out-of-town friends or family in the future. Of course, you will pay for your visitors, but you will be admitted free of charge upon presentation of the enclosed pass.

This is our way of saying "thanks for your interest and support."

Sincerely,

John T. Steiner
President

Throughout its history, Ruby Falls has offered a variety of activities for visitors. Gemstone panning allowed guests to sift and search for gems. The panning structure was built to replicate a sluice, a device that helped miners remove valuable gems or minerals, especially gold, from a slurry of dirt and sand. While no gold was ever discovered at Ruby Falls, pyrite, or fool's gold, was often found while panning.

The Ruby Falls Lantern Tour is a popular, after-hours tour where guests can discover the wonders of the cave illuminated only by hand-held lanterns. Rock formations and shadows take on intriguing dimensions as guides share stories exclusive to this tour. The highlight of the journey takes place when the waterfall is lit with a lantern raised to the ceiling of the cave through a series of pulleys, creating fantastic shadows on the waterfall and cave walls.

As Valentine's Day approaches each year, couples look for unique ways to spend time together. Romance at Ruby offers a romantic twist on the Ruby Falls Lantern Tour. On this special date-night event, guides share the tale of Leo and Ruby Lambert's legendary love story that led to the discovery of the magnificent Ruby Falls. The tour includes a keepsake photograph and a special Valentine's gift. Romance at Ruby tours are very popular and typically sell out every year.

Over millions of years, the force of the waterfall carved out the chamber or dome room of Ruby Falls. This unique space creates an amazing backdrop for private gatherings. Corporate events ranging from dinners to motivational speakers have all taken place next to the subtle roar of the waterfall. Speakers and lighting normally reserved for the waterfall show can be quickly adapted to fit a variety of needs.

Both indoor and outdoor spaces are available to host events at Ruby Falls. With a little Ruby Falls magic and creative flavor, the patios and indoor retail spaces quickly transform into bridal showers and receptions. The historic castle was used as a dance hall in the early days at Ruby Falls.

Haunted Cavern was one of the longest-running events in Ruby Falls history. In the 1980s, Ruby Falls offered an area of the cave not used on tours to the local Jaycees for a haunted event. It became wildly popular, with Ruby Falls still receiving calls about the event 10 years after it closed. In 2004, Ruby Falls reopened Haunted Cavern with much success, and in 2006 joined forces with Fear Connection to create a nationally-recognized, award-winning haunt. Over the years, Haunted Cavern's attendance continued to increase, eventually outgrowing the space in the cave. In 2017, Ruby Falls and Fear Connection moved the haunt to Lookout Valley, opening Dread Hollow, a haunted-town experience. The 20,000-square-foot Dread Hollow venue features a larger capacity, longer operational hours, and space for more intricate theming.

A Town Built on Tainted Soil.

DREAD HOLLOW

DreadHollow.com

Ruby Falls hosts many types of demonstrations and presentations ranging from promotional to educational. From nature to conservancy, Ruby Falls can modify its event spaces to fit any number of themes. Ruby Falls was chosen to be featured on the television series premiere of Scaly Adventures, a family-friendly educational show.

In 1938, Joe Martin rode an Indian Sport motorcycle through Ruby Falls Cavern as a publicity stunt to promote his brother Mickey Martin's thrill show in Chattanooga. Seventy-five years later, Joe's son Robert "Chico" Martin was able to recreate the event riding the same motorcycle through the cave.

While the cave may be 60 degrees year-round, the outdoor facilities do not always share this cool temperature. In order to battle the summer heat, Ruby Falls hosted an ice-cream festival. Young guests at Ruby Falls took part in a scavenger hunt where they sought out ice cream-related clues in the cave. Once they finished their tour, the children could turn in their answers for a free scoop of ice cream. How sweet!

In 2017, the National Caves Association declared June 6 National Day of Caves & Karst. Ruby Falls happily participated in celebrating the holiday, promoting cave conservation and education along with introducing Sammy the Cave Salamander. In 2018, Ruby Falls partnered with the Southeastern Cave Conservancy to further promote the conservation of caves and protection of karst, giving out keychains and magnets.

Racin' at Ruby was an event hosted at Ruby Falls in partnership with Coca-Cola as a salute to NASCAR. The event drew in crowds of car and racing enthusiasts and featured several racing-themed attractions, such as a pit-crew simulator. Guests could compete against professionals as they raced to complete a timed NASCAR tire change, and children raced on themed tricycles to see who was the fastest.

In 1989, Ruby Falls sponsored a Chevrolet Monte Carlo with driver Dale McDowell. McDowell won the ARCA race in Atlanta and went on to compete for the Winston Cup. In 2018, Ruby Falls sponsored Mustang racer Chris Parisi as he made the circuit in the National Mustang Racers Association.

Ruby Falls team members take great pleasure in hosting Battle Below the Clouds, the annual barbecue cook-off where amateur grilling enthusiasts come together to compete for backyard bragging rights for best ribs and pulled pork. The event benefits Lana's Love Foundation, a Chattanooga-based nonprofit organization dedicated to helping pediatric cancer patients and their families have fun. Grillers spend the day at Ruby Falls enjoying great food, good friends, and fun music as they prepare their barbecue. The Lana's Love families are also in attendance, participating in special activities created just for them.

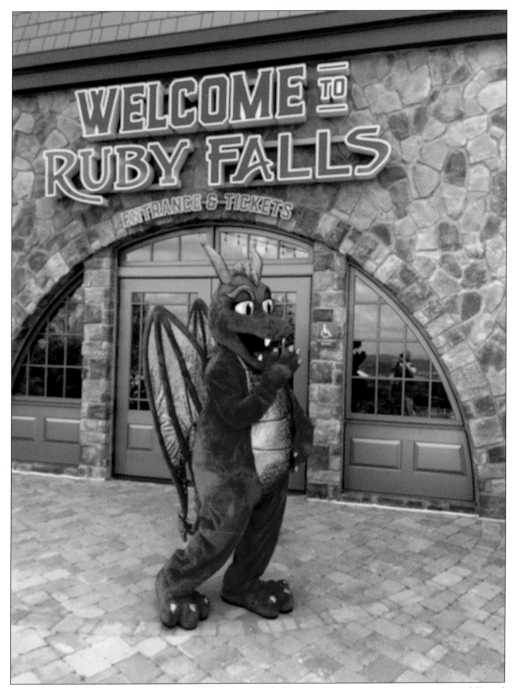

In 2018, Ruby Falls introduced a new ambassador, Ruby the Dragon. Ruby was appointed Royal Guardian of the Cave by the Royal Council of Elders. She lives in the cave and serves as guardian of Ruby Falls Cavern Castle. Ruby is charged to protect the rare beauty of the cave, waterfall, and castle and to uphold the commitment to sustain these natural treasures to share with generations to come.

From 2008 to 2013, Ruby Red Christmas spread holiday cheer at Ruby Falls with old-fashioned yuletide festivities. The iconic castle was decorated with twinkling lights and bows. Storytelling with Mrs. Claus and a special holiday light show at the waterfall delighted guests. A horse-drawn carriage transported riders on a magical journey through the grounds at Ruby Falls for a breathtaking view of the city.

On December 30, 1928, Leo Lambert discovered the magnificent Ruby Falls. Every year on December 30, Ruby Falls celebrates Discovery Day to commemorate this momentous event with special decorations and giveaways. Candles adorn the waterfall room, one for each year since it was discovered, and the first few lucky guests to visit on this day pay the original $2 ticket price. Guests also receive a keepsake postcard and Discovery Day information guide. On the 85th anniversary, Ruby Falls hosted Dancing Under the Stars, a special celebration recreating the dances that were held in the 1930s. The event was open to the public, with dancing, refreshments, and Leo and Ruby lookalikes. Guests were invited to participate in the festivities and tour the cave, where costumed tour guides shared stories and legends of Ruby Falls history.

In 2014, Ruby Falls introduced a new event for the holidays, Ruby Falls Christmas Underground: A Journey to the North Pole. Designed for children and Santa "believers," this event features intricately themed sets, beautiful lights, and costumed actors, creating an immersive experience. A section of the cave not included on the waterfall tour is transformed into the magical mining town of Joystone City. Visitors can help the Joystone miners search for Joystone, a special gemstone that spreads Christmas cheer. Sugar Plum Fairy Village, the Aurora Borealis lights, and a glittering ice cave are just a few of the wonderful sights showcased on this interactive journey to visit Santa Claus.

Five

SUSTAINABILITY AND THE FUTURE

In 2006, John "Jack" Steiner Sr. placed Ruby Falls in a family trust. With a mission to preserve the cave for future generations, Ruby Falls implemented encompassing environmental initiatives. In 2010, Ruby Falls became the first attraction in the United States to earn Green Globe certification, the respected worldwide standard for sustainability. Ruby Falls has become a leader in tourism sustainability and environmentally-sensitive business practices.

The earliest recycling effort at Ruby Falls began in 1928 when the elevator shaft descending deep into Lookout Mountain was excavated. The excavated limestone was used to build the exterior walls of the castle and Lookout Mountain Tower. Stone not used in the castle's construction was placed along the cavern trails in Ruby Falls Cavern and Lookout Mountain Cave.

Reduction of the destination's carbon footprint is an ongoing focus. Ruby Falls was one of the first attractions in the region to provide electric vehicle charging stations. The stations are prominently placed and available to guests and staff. Perks are offered to carpooling Ruby Falls team members.

With no natural light source in the cavern, Ruby Falls was one of the first caves to feature electric lighting. Initially, electricians illuminated the cavern by stringing bare wire with hanging light bulbs. As technology evolved, more effective lighting was installed. In 2009, Ruby Falls began transitioning to LED lighting in the cave, castle, and offices. The energy-efficient lighting is controlled by timers, contributing to a reduction in energy consumption by an estimated 80 percent.

Through grant assistance from the Tennessee Economic and Community Energy Division, Ruby Falls installed an array of solar panels to produce renewable energy. "We are committed to the reduction of our environmental footprint, while providing a better experience for our visitors," explained Ruby Falls president Hugh Morrow when the project was completed. The impact of the solar panels in their first year of use was substantial. In 2009, Ruby Falls saved almost one million pounds of carbon dioxide emissions from entering the atmosphere, the equivalent of offsetting approximately 51,000 gallons of gasoline.

In 2018, Ruby Falls launched a multimillion-dollar expansion, introducing new venues and enhanced guest amenities. Highlighting the natural beauty of Lookout Mountain and Chattanooga, the new venues include the Ruby Falls Ticket Atrium featuring a 37-foot waterfall mural, the expansive Village Gift Shop, accessible Blue Heron Overlook, the Village Plaza, and the Back Porch outdoor dining area with seasonal food carts. Over 18 months of construction, 22,716 tons of rock were excavated and repurposed for other projects. Timed-entry tickets were introduced, replacing hours-long waits. The new ticket process gives guests the flexibility to better plan their visit and enjoy the views and natural beauty of Ruby Falls.

On June 22, 2018, over 300 invited guests attended a grand opening celebration and ribbon-cutting to introduce the newly completed venues. Here, Ruby Falls president Hugh Morrow and Steiner family matriarch Motiva Steiner cut the ceremonial ribbon. Joining them were officials from the state, Chattanooga, and Hamilton County, Steiner family members, the Ruby Falls board of directors, and Jeanne Crawford, granddaughter of Leo Lambert. The morning event was a celebration of the long legacy rising from Leo Lambert's dream and the continuation of Ruby Falls's mission to inspire extraordinary connections to nature through wonder and adventure.

Equally impressive as the appearance of the new venues is what guests do not immediately notice. Energy efficient and water conserving green building techniques were incorporated into the design. The venues were sensitively placed on the land to protect natural habitats, maximizing the amount of natural open space, and storm-water management strategies control the amount of runoff from the site. A 16,000-gallon rainwater collection system is hidden below the plaza for landscape irrigation. Seventy-five percent of construction waste was recycled, and regionally sourced materials were used for landscaping, carpet, drywall, precast concrete, metal roofing, and acoustic ceiling tile.

Opened in June 2018, Ruby Falls Village Gift Shop features over 3,500 square feet of keepsakes and gifts designed to encourage curiosity in caves and geology. The beautiful venue showcases 13 exposed solid-wood trusses. The second-story interior windows are original to the 1929 Ruby Falls Cavern Castle. Open year-round, cave tour admission is not required to explore this specially curated shop.

Ruby Falls was one of 12 scenic overlooks in the state of Tennessee selected by the Tennessee Department of Tourist Development to receive a special viewfinder outfitted with an innovative lens designed to enable guests with color blindness to see a wider range of the vibrant colors of the Tennessee Valley. Especially popular in the fall, the viewers showcase the brilliant hues of the beautiful autumn foliage.

From 2009 to 2018, Ruby Falls ZIPStream Aerial Adventure was a popular attraction. Suspended obstacle courses built in the trees overlooking Chattanooga and the Tennessee River included ladders, nets, walkways, bridges and zip lines. The ZIPStream Adventure Pass featured a 40-foot climbing tower and rushing round-trip zip lines. Reimagined in 2019, Ruby Falls introduced High Point ZIP Adventure, with all new climbing routes on the 40-foot tower and over 700 feet of round-trip rushing zip lines.

Continually striving to improve and set new standards of excellence in tourism and customer satisfaction, Ruby Falls has been recognized for advances in tourism, environmental sustainability, and community involvement. Multiple honors have been presented to Ruby Falls and its team members, including Tennessee Hospitality and Tourism Association's Tourism Managers of the Year, Attraction of the Year, and Community Service Award. In 2018, Ruby Falls president Hugh Morrow was chosen by statewide representatives from the hospitality and tourism industry to receive the prestigious Tennessee Tourism Professional of the Year award. In 2016, Ruby Falls was the first organization in the United States selected for the Green Globe Sustainable Leadership Award. Haunted Cavern, Dread Hollow, and Christmas Underground events have each ranked in the Southeastern Tourism Society's Top 20 within their category for multiple years. Ruby Falls continues to attract interest from print, television, and online publications, garnering accolades such as "10 Best Small City Road Trip Destinations" by Travelocity, "Top 10 Caves in the Nation" by *USA Today*, and "Eleven Most Impressive Waterfalls in the U.S." by Trip Advisor.

For over 89 years, Ruby Falls has proven to be a favorite destination for visitors from across the globe. From the breathtaking underground waterfall hidden deep inside Lookout Mountain to the sweeping views of the Tennessee Valley and Tennessee River, Ruby Falls offers guests the opportunity to discover extraordinary connections to nature through wonder and adventure. Dedicated to protecting the unique geological formations and breathtaking waterfall through sustainability and environmental protection initiatives, Ruby Falls is committed to nurturing these natural wonders for future generations to enjoy.

Discover Thousands of Local History Books
Featuring Millions of Vintage Images

Arcadia Publishing, the leading local history publisher in the United States, is committed to making history accessible and meaningful through publishing books that celebrate and preserve the heritage of America's people and places.

Find more books like this at
www.arcadiapublishing.com

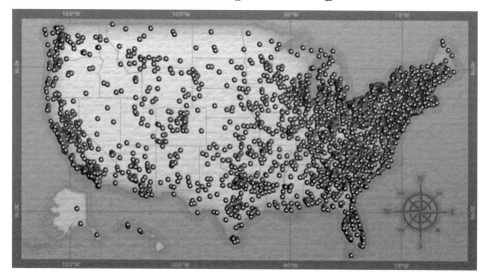

Search for your hometown history, your old stomping grounds, and even your favorite sports team.

Consistent with our mission to preserve history on a local level, this book was printed in South Carolina on American-made paper and manufactured entirely in the United States. Products carrying the accredited Forest Stewardship Council (FSC) label are printed on 100 percent FSC-certified paper.

MADE IN THE USA